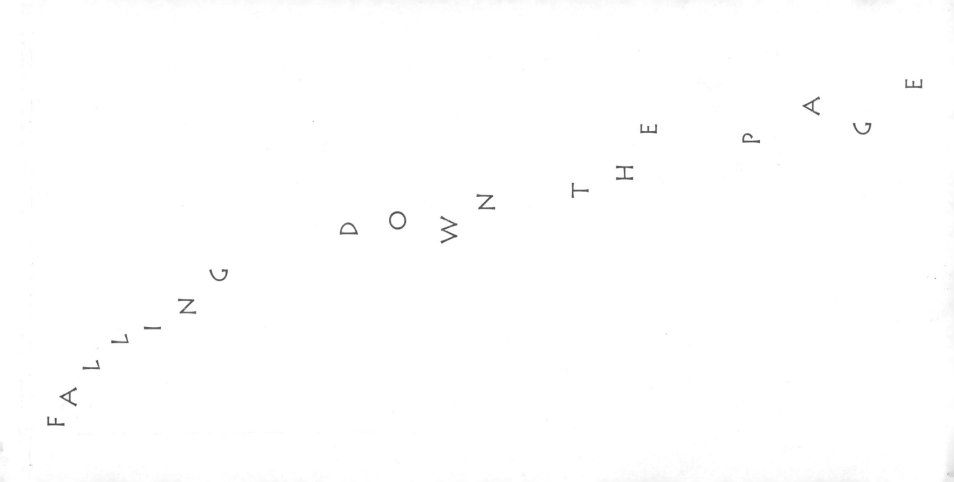

Edited by
GEORGIA
HEARD

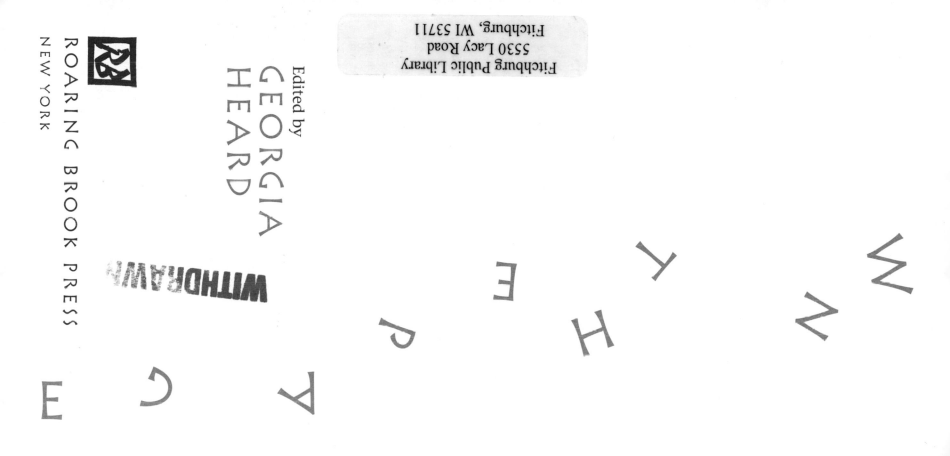

ROARING BROOK PRESS

NEW YORK

Compilation copyright © 2009 by Georgia Heard

Published by Roaring Brook Press

Roaring Brook Press is a division of Holtzbrinck Publishing
Holdings Limited Partnership

175 Fifth Avenue, New York, New York 10010

www.roaringbrookpress.com

Distributed in Canada by H. B. Fenn and Company Ltd.

Library of Congress Cataloging-in-Publication Data
Falling down the page / [compiled] by Georgia Heard. -- 1st ed.
    p. cm.
An anthology of list poems by contemporary poets.
ISBN: 978-1-59643-220-8
1. Children's poetry, American. I. Heard, Georgia.
PS586.3.F33 2008
811'.0080929282--dc22

2007038870

Roaring Brook Press books are available for special promotions
and premiums.
For details contact: Director of Special Markets,
Holtzbrinck Publishers.

First Edition March 2009
Book design by John Grandits
Printed in March 2010 in the United States of America by Worzalla,
Stevens Point, Wisconsin
10 9 8 7 6 5 4 3

For
Rebecca—
thank
you
poetica
friend

And for
Dermot
and Leo—
with
love

CONTENTS

7

INTROD

Out for a walk in New York City I see: yellow cabs speeding down Broadway; people lounging in over-stuffed chairs at a coffee shop. I hear: cars honking; a dog barking in the distance. As I walk along I make a list in my head of what I observe just like Walt Whitman did over one hundred years ago in his famous list poem *Song of Myself.* The list or catalog poem is one of the oldest and most accessible of poetic forms.

We all make lists. We make lists of what we want to do on our summer vacation, lists of friends we want to ask to our birthday party, or lists of books we're eager to read. But does a list make a poem? And what's the difference between a regular what-I-want-to-buy-at-the-candy-store list and a list poem?

Poets meticulously craft their words to create list poems. *Falling Down the Page* highlights the wide variety of the list poem form, from a simple list of words with a twist at the beginning or end to more complicated and detailed descriptive lists. Several list poems combine the list poem form with another poetic form, such as a multiple voice poem as in David Harrison's "Chorus of Four Frogs" or a call-and-response poem in J. Patrick Lewis's "What Is Earth?"

CAUTION

Falling Down the Page sketches the cycle of a school year from summer's end in Eileen Spinelli's "Good-byes" to a no school snow day in "Winter's Presents" by Patricia Hubbell. The poems also trace the arc of an entire school day from "Ways to Greet A Friend" by Avis Harley to end-of-the-day rituals in "Things to Do Today" by Liz Rosenberg.

Not all of the poems in *Falling Down the Page* are specifically about school but they all touch on everyday experiences from throughout the school year. Have you ever looked in your school desk and thought of making a list of all the forgotten treasures inside ("In My Desk" by Jane Yolen)? Perhaps you've found yourself making a list in your head of what you notice as you walk home from school ("Walking Home From School I See:" by Rebecca Kai Dotlich). Or after school, maybe you've made a mental list of what equipment you'll need to go out and skateboard ("Skateboarder" by Sara Holbrook).

After you read a few of these list poems, I bet you'll feel inspired to write one of your own. Think about your day. Jot down what you notice. And let your (list of) words fall down the page.

Happy reading and writing!

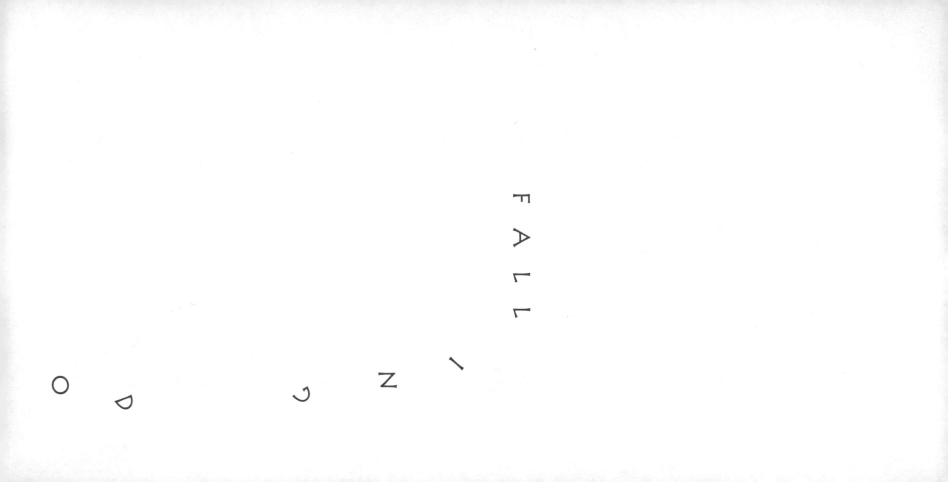

GOOD-BYES

BY EILEEN SPINELLI

It's really hard
to say good-bye
to twinkling beach,
and golden sky,
to castles rising
from the sand,
to Annie's caramel
popcorn stand,
to splashing waves,
to matinees
and indoor games
on rainy days,
to swooping gulls,
and sweeping blue—

but most of all,
dear friend,
to you!

WAYS
TO
GREET
A
FRIEND

BY AVIS HARLEY

Hola is the Spanish *Hello*,
Italians go for *Buon giorno*,

Konichiwa is Japanese,
Bon dia is the Portuguese,

Kalimera when you meet a Greek,
Bonjour is how the French would speak,

Al salaam a'alaykum is the Arabic way,
Apa Khabar they say in Malay.

Ni hao is for the Chinese voice,
Aloha: the Hawaiian choice.

Shalom would be the Hebrew tongue . . . . .
So many ways *Hello* is sung!

ON THE MENU FOR SCHOOL TODAY

Label planets
in our sky.
Learn how numbers
multiply.
Count coins.
String beads.
Shake bells.
Plant seeds.
Map constellations
dot
      to
            dot. . . .
Decorate
a flowerpot.
Say a poem.
Spell b-u-t-t-e-r-f-l-y.
Shout hello.
Wave good-bye.

BY REBECCA KAI DOTLICH

1

They've canceled recess,
time to play.
Instead it's
clear-out-desks
today.
Though all I've got
is junk
in there.
So let *them* clean it—
I don't care.

2

Inside they'll find
one
holey
sock,

3

the insides of
a broken clock,
a bag of feathers,
three brown stones,
a pair of moldy
old pinecones,
my last year's textbook,

4

DESK

tons of tests
all marked in red,
a blue jay's nest,
a note from
Mary Ellen White,
my braces that were
much too tight,
a lunch box
with a great big
hunk
of rotting cheese.
You see—
just junk.

No—wait—
each piece
can tell a tale.
It's not just
junk
that's old and stale.
I'll do that
cleaning out,
you see
each piece of junk's
my history.

BY JANE YOLEN

SHOW-AND-TELL ROCKS

BY TERRY WEBB HARSHMAN

I collect rocks.
All kinds of rocks:
little rocks, big rocks—
rocks by the box;

fossil rocks, lava rocks,
mica and shale;
camp rocks and cave rocks—
rocks by the pail;

fool's gold and geodes
and flint arrowheads;
pebbles and pudding stones—
rocks in the shed;

meteor rocks
that tumbled through space;
moonstones and marble—
rocks by the case.

If rocks could talk,
the secrets we'd hear!
Rocks have been rocking
for MILLIONS of years!

I have rocks in my pockets
and rocks in my socks.
Rocks are forever—
I collect rocks.

IN MY HAND

BY MARILYN SINGER

I like to hold in my hand

a baseball,

a shell,

a fistful of sand,

a feather,

a letter,

a red rubber band.

Things that tickle,

Things that trickle.

Things to snap and toss and fold

or just hold.

HELPING HANDS

BY ALLAN WOLF

Hands are for taking.
Hands are for holding.
Hands are for shaping
and paper plane folding.

Hands are for grasping.
Hands are for shaking.
Hands are for touching
and shadow-play making.

Hands are for dressing,
buttoning, zipping.
Scrambling, buttering,
flapper-jack flipping.

Hands are for clapping,
juggling, jiggling.
Hands are for washing
and brushing and wiggling.

Hands are for raising,
writing and talking.
Catching and throwing
and bright sunlight blocking,
wringing and twisting
and turning and knocking.
Clock hands are perfect
for ticking and tocking.
But upside-down acrobat hands
are for walking.

CLAY PLAY

BY KRISTINE O'CONNELL GEORGE

Pound it, round it,
stretch it, roll it,
braid or bowl it,
mold it, fold it.

Press it flat
and very thin
for daisy petals—
fishes' fin.

Take a lump
(a good-sized chunk)
for oak tree stump
or elephant trunk.

Is it crooked?
Not quite right?

Pound it, round it,
stretch it, roll it,
braid or bowl it,
Fold it, mold it,
until you see
what it *really* wants to be.

CREATIVITY

BY EILEEN SPINELLI

An artist takes:

colored pencil
piece of yarn
wooden slat from
some old barn
sidewalk chalk
or spool of wire
can of paint
or junkyard tire
twig or twine
or river rock
seed or seashell
woolen sock
bar of soap
or paper heart
and turns it
happily
to art.

Perhaps you have:
a shard of plate
a hinge from someone's
garden gate
a scrap of quilt
or rusty screw . . .

then you can be
an artist too.

THINGS TO DO IF YOU ARE A PENCIL

BY ELAINE MAGLIARO

Be sharp.

Wear a slick yellow suit

and a pink top hat.

Tap your toes on the tabletop,

listen for the right rhythm,

then dance a poem

across the page.

RECIPE FOR WRITING AN AUTUMN POEM

BY GEORGIA HEARD

One teaspoon wild geese.
One tablespoon red kite.
One cup wind song.
One pint trembling leaves.
One quart darkening sky.
One gallon north wind.

WHY POETRY?

BY LEE BENNETT HOPKINS

Why poetry?
Why?

Why sunsets?
Why trees?

Why birds?
Why seas?

Why you?
Why me?

Why friends?
Why families?

Why laugh?
Why cry?

Why hello?
Why good-bye?

Why poetry?
That's why!

WORDS IN MY PILLOW

BY NAOMI SHIHAB NYE

I hide words inside my pillowcase.
Words that taste good—

MONKEY.
COZY.
POUCH.

No one can see them
but I find them waiting for me.
Like the TUMMY hiding inside my body.
No one can see it
but I know what's in there—

MUFFIN
WHIPPED CREAM
PEACHES
BLUEBERRIES
TORTILLA
CHEESE

YUMMIES are in there.
Mashed POTATO is in there.

The words are playing together
when I am saying or thinking them.

YES
RIPE
PURPLE
WOOSH!
is in my pillow.

My friends the words
go to bed before I do.
But they never
go away.

BOOKTIME

BY AVIS HARLEY

So many places to read a book—
bedroom
living room
kitchen nook

classroom
lunchroom
library
hall—
bus stop
treetop
hilltop
mall

backyard
garden
patio
park—
under-
the-sheets-
in-flash-lit-
dark

teahouse
treehouse
subway
train—
attic
camper
trailer
plane

seaside
lakeside
by a brook—
Where do you like to read your book?

ARE WE THERE YET?

BY HEIDI ROEMER

Ocean maps,
Weather maps,
Maps that chart the stars.

Road maps,
Train maps
Show us where we are.
Builder's maps,
Landscape maps,
Maps drawn in the sand.

Fold-up maps,
Rolled-up maps.
A globe held in my hand.

Tattered maps,
Treasure maps—
What secrets are they holding?

I like maps.
I read maps.
They get me where I'm going.

LOST AND FINDS

BY REBECCA KAI DOTLICH

This box holds treasures;
all shapes,
all kinds,
dig deep—
look twice!
For lost

and finds . . . .

A poodle pin.
A daisy ring.
One silver yo-yo
without a string.

One baseball cap.
A spoon.
A comb.
One yellow boot.
A note from home.

A plastic umbrella.
A letter.
A sock.
Two blue shoelaces.
One bicycle lock.

A photograph.
One bag of beads.
Things that someone
looks for,
needs.

A charm,
a key,
a pair of gloves—
something
someone
misses,
loves.

TEST DAY

BY KATHI APPELT

It's never about the things I know:

Where the old turtle hid her eggs
How many homeruns my brother hit last season
My mom's favorite colors—violet and pink
That chocolate chip cookies need vanilla
The year my grandfather fought in the war
The year he didn't come back
That my great-great-aunt learned to drive when she was 68
What time the moon rose last night
And what time it set this morning
How the thunder scares my ginger-striped cat
Why the neighbor's hound howls at stars
Where the grackle built her nest
What to put in my dad's cup of coffee . . .

It's never about the things I know.

WHAT IS EARTH?

BY J. PATRICK LEWIS

What is earth, whale?
A sea where I sing.
What is earth, robin?
A thing I call Spring.
What is earth, python?
A space to squeeze in.
What is earth, penguin?
A place to freeze in.
What is earth, camel?
A land without water.
What is earth, housefly?
No spot for a swatter.
What is earth, earthworm?
An apple a day.
What is earth, groundhog?
A hole in PA.
What is earth, eagle?
A sky where I soar.
What is earth, cockroach?
A house I explore.
What is earth, eel?
It's really quite shocking.
What is earth, parrot?
Where I go on talking

and talking
and talking
and talking....

SPINNERS

BY MARILYN SINGER

A wheel.
A top.
A carousel.
A dryer full of clothes.
A yo-yo twirling on a string.
A dancer on her toes.
A lazy leaf caught on a breeze.
An egg before you peel it.
A ceiling fan.
A tall red stool.
The Earth—but we can't feel it.

THINGS TO DO IF YOU ARE THE SUN

BY BOBBI KATZ

Let planets loop around you.
Be Earth's very own star.
Keep things warm enough for people.
Keep things cool enough for penguins.
Slip away to end the day.
Light the moon at night.
Let people and animals sleep.
And at the crack of dawn,
wake up the world!

WINTER'S PRESENT

BY PATRICIA HUBBELL

Feathers for the sky
New clothes for bare branches
Pom-poms for the fences
Top hats for the mailboxes
Silver spears for house eaves
Blossoms for the windowpanes
Quilts for parked cars
Stars for all mittens
—And for the children?
No school!

JUST LOOK!

BY VALISKA GREGORY

A cardinal in red velvet,
two doves in stylish gray,
four sparrows dressed in tattered brown,
a loud-mouth bully of a jay,

a foxy squirrel in brown-gold fur,
a chipmunk with cheeks bulged fat,
and in the maple tree a crow
as calm as a monk in black,

a nuthatch skittering down the trunk,
and gossiping grackles below—
we see their trick-track twiggy feet
write messages in snow.

Our gifts of thistle, millet, seed,
seem small under endless sky,
but watching them feast, our hearts are full,
as if we too might fly.

TREE SONG

BY GEORGE ELLA LYON

Roots,
trunk,
branches,
leaves.
As a tree
gives
so it
receives:
food
from
the earth,
rain
and sun
from
the sky.
Its roots
reach
deep
and its crown
rises
high.
Blossoms
in spring,
fruit
in summer
and fall:
home
for many,
shelter
for all.

OAK TREE

BY GEORGIA HEARD

Sky
Touching
Up
Up
Up
Reaching
Up
Up
Up
Up
Climbs
Acorn
Small
One

(To be read bottom to top)

BY REBECCA KAI DOTLICH

A bus with a flat tire.
Pennies in a puddle.
Baby birds.
Fat worms.
A pair of pigeons.
A crooked gate.
A mailbox spray-painted pink.
A bulldog wearing a raincoat.
A bumblebee.
A reflection
in a window—
me!

CHORUS OF FOUR FROGS
BY DAVID HARRISON

1ST VOICE	2ND VOICE	3RD VOICE	4TH VOICE
			Ker-plum!
Greedeep	Ribbet?		Ker-plum!
Greedeep	Ribbet?	Peep-peep	Ker-plum!
Greedeep		Peep-peep	
Greedeep		Peep-peep	
Greedeep	Ribbet?	Peep-peep	Ker-plum!
Greedeep	Ribbet?	Peep-peep	Ker-plum!
Greedeep	Ribbet?	Peep-peep	Ker-plum!
Greedeep	Ribbet?	Peep-peep	Ker-plum!
			Ker-plum!
Greedeep	Ribbet?	Peep-peep	
Greedeep	Ribbet?	Peep-peep	
		Peep-peep	
Greedeep		Peep-peep	
Greedeep			Ker-plum!
Greedeep	Ribbet?		Ker-plum!
Greedeep	Ribbet?		
Greedeep			

SKATEBOARDER

BY SARA HOLBROOK

Wood pusher.
Curb jumper.
Helmet head.
I could be
sittin' safe inside, instead
wrist guards,
kneepads,
scuffed-up jeans,
driveway tricks,
and half-pipe dreams.
Soften knees,
duck, jump, drop,
kick-it, big spin.
Hope! Believe.
Grabbing air,
ollie, slide.
Each rail, each ramp
a high-risk ride.
Practicing
first light 'til late.
Foot pumper.
Stair bumper.
Born to skate.

UNDER MY BED

BY HEIDI STEMPLE

Under my bed
a party rocks
with dust bunnies and unmatched socks.

The guests line up
to do-si-do
two by two and heel to toe—

A stuffed brown bear
with a missing ear,
a mitten knit with
a red reindeer.

A shoestring,
and a candy cane,
my sweater with the grape juice stain.

My favorite blanket
I thought I lost
and a sneaker that I must have tossed.

The book I was reading
but didn't like
and the seat from my cousin's ten-speed bike.

And, though my guests have had lots of fun,
it's cleaning day—
this party's done!

MESSAGE FROM THE MOON

BY LARA ANDERSON

Moon breathes
slumber over cities,
fire hydrants,
sweeping rivers,

a rooftop terrace,
a puddle
that shivers.

Its tender light
threads,
weaves
over alleyways,
cafe eaves,
stone cathedrals,

corner clocks,
peeks
through windows
of bakery shops.

On cloudless nights,
its polished light
settles on sailboats,
seacoasts,
a cabled bridge . . . .

Moon's message
f
a
l
l
s,
whispers
. . . *hush* . . . .

SHOOTING STAR

BY AVIS HARLEY

at my window

in the night

a shooting star

silver-white

a sudden streak

a bright surprise

a falling fire

a light that dies

a fleeting gift

a blaze to keep

a wishing time

before I sleep . . .

WHILE YOU ARE SLEEPING, SCHOOL . . .

BY REBECCA KAI DOTLICH

Turns on a light,
sighs goodnight
to bulletin boards,
cubbies,
books.

Yawns,
looks
at poems dangling
on paper trees,
cut-out bees,
notebooks,
totes.

Dreams
of coats,
boots,
shuffling of shoes,
friends whispering
in twos . . .

the rattle
of spelling words,
the scratching
of pencils,

a friendship song,
a jumping jack,
buses bringing
children back.

THINGS TO DO TODAY

BY LIZ ROSENBERG

Open eyes, check for sunlight.
Get feet somehow from bed to floor.
Brush teeth, spit. Greet
That girl in the mirror. Stretch.
Pick a color for the day. Wear it.
Pick a flavor. Eat it.
Get from kitchen to front door,
Down
The
Steps. Hold on tight.
Remember to jump the last step.
Learn something
Good. Make someone feel
Better. Try to
Make someone laugh out loud.
Watch for dark blue, then darkness.
Wait for the moon. It waited for you.
Eat your favorite thing before bed.
Brush teeth, spit. Say good-night
To that girl in the mirror.
Get feet back into bed.
Check for moonlight. Starlight. Weather.
Read before sleep,
Remember a good thing that happened.
Forget a not-so-good one.
Tomorrow you get to do it all again.
Lucky you! Don't watch the clock. Just
Dream.